THE LANDSCAPES OF
Essex

STAN JARVIS & ROBERT HALLMANN

COUNTRYSIDE BOOKS

First published 2000
Photographs © Robert Hallmann 2000
Text © Stan Jarvis 2000
Reprinted 2003

COUNTRYSIDE BOOKS
3 CATHERINE ROAD
NEWBURY, BERKSHIRE

To view our complete range of books,
please visit us at
www.countrysidebooks.co.uk

ISBN 1 85306 646 X

Pictures – page 1 – the Thames from
Two-Tree Island, Leigh-on-Sea,
page 4 – Maldon and page 80 –
Stansgate, near Steeple.

Designed by Mon Mohan
Produced through MRM Associates Ltd., Reading
Printed in Singapore

Contents

INTRODUCTION

'If I were called upon to choose between beauty and truth, I should not hesitate; I should hold to beauty, being confident that it bears within it a truth both higher and deeper than truth itself ...', so says Anatole France.

In looking through the following photographs and the descriptive annotations I hope you will understand my reasons for choosing these particular places to demonstrate my admiration of the county in which I have lived and worked for more than 50 years.

Many people, including fortunate natives of this county, have spoken to me at book-signings and talks I have given all over Essex. Whilst the majority show an understandable pride in the county of their birth, I have heard some misconceptions expressed such as: 'Essex is flat'; 'Essex is all houses and no trees'; and, as wrong as it is offensive, 'Essex is over-populated, all suburbs and no villages.'

The photographs in this book will show how wrong such statements are. Beauty, 'the smile of God' as the poet has it, can be discovered all over Essex in a climate that is as kind to man and his animals as it is to the woods and pastures. And he can trace wonderful walks along lanes and through fields and woods now preserved for the use and enjoyment of future generations in a county still beautiful in its old age.

Through these images by an expert photographer, supported by my comments and descriptions, I hope you will enjoy making a new acquaintance with Essex as it can still be found in this 21st century.

Stan Jarvis

ESSEX

I go through the fields of blue water
On the south road of the sea:
High to north the East country
Holds her green fields to me,
For she that I gave over
Gives not over me.

Last night I lay at Good Easter
Under a hedge I knew;
Last night in wood by High Easter
I trod the May-floors blue:
Out of the sea the sun came
Bidding me wake and rue ...

England has greater counties,
Their peace to hers is small,
Low hills, rich fields, calm rivers!
In Essex, seek them all –
Essex, where I that found them
Did but lose them all!

Arthur Shearley Cripps,
a returning missionary,
on SS *Goorkha*, May 1906

West Thurrock and West Tilbury

West Thurrock's history and development are told in this one photograph (*opposite*). From the ancient church on the hill to the modern 'soap factory' which now looms over it. As Pevsner, the architectural expert says of this church of St Clement: 'The most remarkable thing about the church is its position, lovely and rather forlorn in the marshes, cut off by the railway from the village and now overtowered by a modern factory (Proctor and Gamble) just east of it.'

It is an inspiring sight, looking out across the marshes to the Thames, even if industry has penetrated to its very doorstep. There is still the green-ness of the marshes to contrast with St Clement's 600-year-old tower with diagonal buttresses decorated in layers of stonework interspersed with bands of flints. Will that factory beside it last for 500 years? But then, it is purely functional and mass-productive and must change to suit consumer demand. This factory, which began production in 1940, was the first soapmaking plant to use the totally enclosed continuous process based on the 'hydrolyzer', to produce such well known brands as Ariel, Daz, Flash and so on. This juxtaposition of cleanliness and godliness is indicative of the importance of the area as a whole. As an Urban District of local government it was the largest in England.

Tilbury is best known for its docks now, but we see on the Ordnance Survey map that Tilbury Fort is clearly marked as a 'Non-Roman' antiquity. It was completed in 1683, after 13 years, to counter any ideas an enemy might have had of sailing an invasion fleet up the Thames to London. It was largely rebuilt in the middle of the 19th century, but the experts tell us it remains in plan as it was built, 'a very rare example in this country of the bastioned system of defence in depth which includes ... a double line of moats on the landward side'.

One could say that such an example of military might would tend to put in the shade the humble parish church of West Tilbury, but it is the diminutive size of St James and its position on the edge of the escarpment looking down over the Thames (*inset*) which make such an impact. Its windows show it was originally early Norman. The tower, built in 1883, shows the parishioners' continuing, loving care.

South Benfleet and Thundersley

A copy of the *Official Guide to Benfleet Urban District*, published in 1972, tells us: 'There are two ancient inns in South Benfleet, the Anchor and the Hoy and Helmet. Both were probably built in the early 16th century and both still display original oak beams and other timber mouldings and carvings.

Externally the Hoy and Helmet has a charming half-timbered front with a many gable-tiled roof and is scheduled as a building of architectural importance … the Crown has a foundation probably as old … but the original inn was taken down at the beginning of the last century and the present brick-built one erected in its place.' After a lorry demolished part of the Crown, which stands facing the Hoy and Helmet (*opposite*) the locals,

with a nice touch of humour, voted for a change of name and it became the Half Crown!

The two inns were first built when the wide-spreading forest of Essex had shrunk but little from its original coverage of this whole area. The existing copse called Shipwright's Wood stands as the evidence that the forest provided the skeletons and planking of many a gallant ship of the line. In our age, though, the Downs, on the edge of the ridge above the Thames, has been preserved as a public open space of some 400 acres.

From there the view across the creek to Canvey Island is a changing panorama as the tide ebbs and flows. And, despite industrialisation further up the Thames, this is a bird-watcher's paradise, a chance to see rarities like greenshanks and spoonbills as well as gulls in all their variety.

The parish church of St Peter, Thundersley (*inset*) continues the association with shipbuilding in that the timber tower has some old ship's beams in its construction. It is a history book of this ancient settlement in the forest. The roof is an amazing construction covering nave and aisles, ending just six feet from the ground. One of the church's three bells dates from 1588. The stained glass windows of the modern extension illustrate the life of its patron saint, Peter. This extension, made necessary by the huge increase in the population of the parish, was consecrated by the Bishop of Chelmsford in 1966.

Leigh-on-Sea

The fishing industry at Leigh is mentioned in the Domesday Book of 1086. Centuries later, the long, narrow creek reaching up to the quay at Old Leigh formed a naval base to hold and service the fleet which Admiral Blake assembled here in the 17th century. So the countless ships and boats which proudly claim Leigh as their home port keep up that great British tradition of brave seafarers in peace and war.

It was after 1700 that the fishermen of Leigh began to develop the oyster trade by laying down oyster beds. At the end of the 18th century the growing fashion for sea-bathing started the building here of one or two hotels but by 1800, South End (i.e. of Prittlewell) became the favoured site for further building and so Leigh reverted to its role of sailing capital of the south-east.

In the days around the opening of the 19th century the humble shrimp brought prosperity to the growing village. From the building of 'bawleys', boats of no more than six feet draught, to their fitting out with a huge spread of sail, prosperity blessed the harbour; morning and evening the billowing sails were a spectacle as they raced each other to and from the shrimping grounds in the Thames estuary. The Peter Boat inn was named after the patron saint of those hardy fishermen. Some of those same fishermen gave a boost to that other industry of our island race – smuggling! As a fleet they could easily outwit the manoeuvres of the Revenue men as they struggled to confiscate the foreign goods and liquor which for the fishermen were 'a nice little earner'. Today the sailing is largely for fun, but shrimp-boats still put into the quay with their shrimps boiled in a big copper on board while making the passage home.

Hadleigh Castle and Canvey Island

'By far the most important later medieval castle in the county', says Sir Nikolaus Pevsner in his *Buildings of England* series, Essex volume. On the low-lying edge of Hadleigh, overlooking Benfleet Creek, Canvey Island and the Thames beyond it, the stump of the tower (*opposite*) still rises powerfully against the sky, as Constable captured it in his inspiring painting. What a history it has!

It was built of Kentish ragstone around 1230 for Hubert de Burgh, and rebuilt a century or so later. Sad to say, a landslide carried away the main residential building to the south. The tallest part now to be seen is the south-east tower. It still has the power to catch the imagination with its three towers and its ruins, 'as cut off from their environment as they are cut off from contemporary life,' as one guide book aptly puts it.

Born as a mere island of silt in the Thames, moving at the whim of tides and currents, Canvey Island was preserved through the engineering genius of Dutchmen under Cornelius Vermuyden who finished their work in 1623. Until the opening of the 20th century Canvey was used as fields in which to graze sheep and cattle with a twice-a-year fair, so there are very few old buildings. One of them, though, is the 17th-century Lobster Smack inn of typical Essex clapboard timber construction. Local people tell you with pride that it is mentioned in Charles Dickens' *Great Expectations*.

In our own day Canvey suffered a traumatic experience at nature's hand in 1953 when three abnormally high tides through night and day from 1st February swept clear across the Island, flooding more than 12,000 homes and drowning countless farm animals. Canvey recovered from that awful flood and is a happy and refreshing place for islanders and tourists alike. Viewed from Hadleigh Downs at night, Canvey Island is a mass of twinkling lights (*inset*).

Prittlewell and Thorpe Bay

Prittlewell (*opposite*) is perhaps best known as the parish that gave birth to the famous seaside town of Southend. The 'child' was born when a 'Pleasant Row' of cottages was built down by the broadening Thames estuary, so that visitors could take the 'sea-bathing' which was becoming fashionable in the 1760s. It is amazing how quickly the 'South End' of Prittlewell expanded to cater for the thousands who began to flock there throughout the summer months. In 1830 a pier was constructed and it was extended in 1846, making it the longest in the world.

Roles were reversed and Southend developed into a large county borough whilst Prittlewell survived as a mere adjunct to one of the most important towns in south-east England. Southend offers all the features of a large and busy coastal resort, from an art gallery to a pleasure park. When visitors catch sight of the tower of St Mary's church standing proudly at the crossroads in Prittlewell, they know that the beach and its many attractions are just around the corner.

Thorpe Bay (*inset*) at the eastern end of Southend is a dormitory town for folk who are drawn to wide, airy skies within sight and sound of the sea as it surges and retreats up

the wide Thames estuary. Here, on the north bank of this famous river, the dramatic skyscapes of winter give way to the blue skies of summer as locals and visitors alike relax at the water's edge.

Battlesbridge

'... the lovely unexpected village of Battlesbridge, where, suddenly, in the middle of the inland landscape, arise the masts and brown, close-furled sails of some sea-and-river-going barge.'

James Agate, *Ego2* (1936)

It sounds warlike, but it isn't. This hamlet of Rettendon gets its name from the local 'lord' mentioned in records of the early 14th century, Reginald Bataille. He was of a family of landowners who had a bridge built across the creek, an upper reach of the River Crouch. Centuries earlier, King Canute is said to have anchored his boats here when his army sallied forth to beat the Saxons under Edmund Ironside at the Battle of Assandun (Ashingdon), five miles or so to the east.

The first mill to stand astride the creek here was a tidal mill because the River Crouch was not flowing strongly enough to turn a millwheel. A medieval man of vision got gangs of men together to embank the creek and so create a head of water at each full tide which then turned the wheel on the ebb. In the 18th century the mill was rebuilt with four pairs of stones on separate floors to grind the barge-loads of grain brought from Essex farms round the coast and up the creek. The original tidal mill was destroyed by fire around the 1930s and a steam one built by Mr Matthews a little later, so making it independent of tide and time.

Industry has left Battlesbridge, the hamlet has been bypassed by the A130 and traffic has been reduced to a trickle. Though it has to be said that more than one smuggler has tried to creep up the creek in the dead of night to unload a loathsome cargo of drugs, or drinks, and then to slip away on the outgoing tide. The quiet street now offers easy access to an antiques centre – some 70 dealers in five fine old buildings offer items of an age in keeping with their surroundings. Two pubs, the Harp and the Barge, stand at either end of the hamlet offering refreshment and an agreeable stroll between them.

South Woodham Ferrers

A new town sprang up in rural Essex — a town which still preserves the atmosphere and the pleasures of the countryside. It was the brainchild of the County Council who acquired 1,300 acres here to set up an area for development which aimed at providing well-built homes for some 18,000 people with plenty of open space around it. Her Majesty Queen Elizabeth II opened the Town Square in 1981. This is where the shops and businesses congregate, but just outside the limits of this little town is Marsh Farm Country Park, where a working farm encourages visits by local schools. Here they can feed the animals and watch various farming displays, depending on the season. The park also boasts a visitors' centre, an adventure playground, picnic areas and delightful walks along the River Crouch.

It is low tide — we can dare to negotiate the ford from Woodham Ferrers and look forward to Hullbridge (*opposite*). Traffic down the Crouch these days is almost entirely for pleasure as, with bellying sails or churning screws, little boats push hard against the tide or run free with the current to the open sea. They all have to pass Bridgemarsh Island. This was embanked by one hopeful sheep farmer a century or more ago but well before the

Second World War an extra high tide broke through that embankment and wreaked havoc. Since when, Bridgemarsh has been left in lonely, marshy solitude.

North Fambridge

Sail up the Crouch on a sunny day. As you pass Althorne Creek on your starboard side you come to Bridgemarsh Island and further on North Fambridge, two or three miles upriver. 'Drains' excavated to take the water off the low-lying land, along with huge ponds from old gravel workings and the like, restrict this small village to the space between the Crouch to the south and the railway to the north.

A fascinating old County Guide, written by Miller Christy in 1887 tells us North Fambridge is: 'A small, secluded and marshy parish on the north side of the River Crouch, across which there is a ferry to South Fambridge.' The population then was just 142 souls. Given the large families of the day you can see that there were not many houses. As to that ferry; though there are slipways below the village on the north bank there is no sign of a ferry operating here today. But there is that old public house on the river bank, still called, nostalgically, the Ferry Boat Inn.

Blue House Farm, at the eastern end of the parish, is unspoilt marshland with a special place in the fauna of Essex because the whole area of the farm was bought by the Essex Wildlife Trust in 1998 to provide 600 acres which are home to increasing numbers of Brent geese, pintail and shoveller ducks. There is every hope that otters will return to this isolated haven. It is through the winter months that the migrants can best be seen.

Everything about North Fambridge seems to be small.

The small church of the Holy Trinity has a small wooden belfry with one small bell in it. It is hard to believe that this rather lonely little place has been sheltering people since 1556 at least, for that is the date of the first entry in the parish register.

Burnham-on-Crouch

There's an international air about dear old Burnham. Boats big and small come up river to the quay for a day of rest and resupply and what an interesting sight they make for the landlubber taking that lovely stroll along the river front. Just to be in the hustle and bustle of sailors speaking all the languages of Europe is a fascination while the varied activities of the quayside and the sights and smells of this little port on the River Crouch are added pleasures.

The town grew from a riverbank settlement so early on that the parish church shows lots of 14th century architecture. The font is actually more than 800 years old. What generations of babies have proudly borne the names they were given in Burnham-on-Crouch!

The most interesting walk is all along the quay from the museum and the Royal Burnham Yacht Club at the west end, to the Royal Corinthian Yacht Club at the east end. One can return via the mainly Georgian High Street with its unusual Victorian brick, octagonal clock tower. Two inscriptions tell the story: 'Burnham Charity Trust — These schools were enlarged AD 1863', and, 'This clock and tower were added to the schools by public subscription in memory of Laban Sweeting AD 1877'.

There's a hard luck story associated with the Long Row in the town. Twenty-four houses all built under one long roof of slate! It was put up to the order of John Smith, an oyster merchant, to house the crews of his boats. That roof had to be replaced after the awful damage of the hurricane of the 1980s, which rushed through Burnham.

Tillingham and Mayland

One landowner in this village is no less than St Paul's Cathedral. In fact, it is the oldest of all their estates. They obtained it from King Ethelbert before AD 616. The weatherboarded cottages, all painted white, add to the real beauty of the place (*inset*). Many of them were built in 1880 by St Paul's to fit suitably into the village scene. The *Shire County Guide* sums it all up: 'The time to see Tillingham in all its glory is the day of the flower show in July when market stalls crowd the green, the inns are open all day and celebrations continue into the night.'

The church, with its strongly-buttressed 14th-century western tower, seen against a verdant backcloth of trees is a picture to calm the nerves and recharge the flagging spirit. For 600 years it has stood there, at times neglected but patiently awaiting the love of succeeding generations; recording true parish history through baptisms, marriages and burials – a place for reflection on, and silent thanks for, God's benefactions.

Mayland parish, along with its modern neighbour, Maylandsea, is situated just south of Lawling Creek. The creek was fashioned in pre-history as the River Chelmer made its junction with the Blackwater and the great, grey North Sea.

It is not surprising that in modern times plant nurseries have grown ever larger to cater for the gardening passions of an increasingly affluent society. The Mayland Mill (*opposite*) is an inn offering solid and liquid refreshment to the gardeners from miles around who like to rest and refresh themselves after their tour of the local nurseries looking for just the right plant for their plot. Who do we have to thank for laying the foundations of this gardening mecca? A humble gardener by the name of Thomas Smith. Back in the 1930s he invested all his savings in eleven acres of land here. And he it was who started all those glasshouse crops – tomatoes, cucumbers, lettuces and strawberries. In 1909 he had written a book on gardening and in 1935 it was still being published in revised editions! By the time he died in 1955, aged 98, he had been awarded the Veitch Memorial Gold Medal by the Royal Horticultural Society.

Bradwell

Or, Bradwell-juxta-Mare as the oldest records in Latin put it, is a long name for a small village. But in recent years it has taken up a good many columns in the newspapers because it was chosen as the site for a nuclear power station which has provided power for the national electricity grid since 1963. The difference in age between it and the parish church is all of 1,300 years!

The power station offers a complete tour to suit children and adults alike. It includes an exhibition of man's discovery of electricity and of its uses in this modern age. To remind us of our natural Essex heritage it also provides a nature trail in its wide-spreading grounds. How that brooding grey bulk contrasts with the village itself, on the Blackwater estuary where, at Bradwell Waterside, many a mariner has set sail in his frail craft for faraway places.

In the village just down the road to the south, off the B1021, there are other points of interest. One of them is Bradwell Lodge, lived in by Sir Henry Bate Dudley and, more recently, by the late Tom Driberg, MP. Its unusual belvedere or one might say 'a room with a view' which tops the roof was the work of Robert Adam, the 18th-century architect. Its extension is by John Johnson the architect who also designed Chelmsford's Shire Hall.

The Church of St Thomas the Apostle, with its 14th-century nave, was much restored in 1864. Its churchyard is framed by houses of various ages in a charming juxtaposition which would challenge any architectural historian.

That parish church in the village is upstaged in age and interest by St Peter's-on-the-Wall, which is actually on the sea wall one and a half miles to the north-east. Nikolaus Pevsner, proclaimed authority on the buildings of England, tells us, 'It is in all probability the very church built by St Cedd *c.* 654. It consists now of nothing but the nave, but the existence of a west porch and an aisled chancel as wide as the nave have been ascertained …' Pictures cannot capture the strong feelings aroused when visiting this tiny chapel but like the photograph below they can give some idea of its lonely situation.

Epping Forest and High Beech

The last remnant of that great forest which in ancient times covered the whole of eastern England, lingers on around the town of Epping. As settlers moved in and families proliferated, the forest was reduced and ultimately divided into the two entities now named after Epping and Hainault. They suffered through their proximity to these places to the extent that, in 1848, Parliament proposed that both areas be split amongst the local landowners and that they be developed for housing and industrial purposes.

Hainault Forest went that way, and was developed, but Epping Forest was saved through the public outcry led by Thomas Willingale, a humble old village labourer. He had always obtained his firewood from the forest, a traditional right afforded to the dwellers there. When the forest was fenced off for development he simply broke down that fence and persisted in his ancient right to lop trees. He was prosecuted and evicted from his cottage. This rallied all the villagers and brought help from important people with influence. The strength of their protest stirred the City of London to buy all the forest area remaining in private hands; their enquiries in 1871 showed that the forest then covered 3,021 acres. By 1880 the City had appointed a board of Forest Rangers to manage all aspects of the newly constituted Epping Forest. The photograph opposite shows two of the Forest's well known inhabitants – Bigfoot and Gulliver!

Off Rangers Road, Chingford, stands Queen Elizabeth's Hunting Lodge, beautiful in its own right and also historical because it was actually used by Henry VIII to watch the hunt or to shoot at deer driven before him. Today the interior has displays which enlarge upon the Forest in general and the Lodge in particular.

Alfred, Lord Tennyson, lived at Beech House for three years from 1837, enjoying the rural peace where he felt inspired to write his *In Memoriam*. It is surprising how peaceful the place still is despite its closeness to London and the traffic that engenders. The church at High Beech (*inset*), dedicated to the Holy Innocents, was rebuilt in 1873, of stone, with a tall and slender spire which complements, gracefully, the trees growing all about, a good example of the work of Sir Arthur Blomfield in his 'Gothic Revival' style. The 13 bells in its steeple are played by a carillon.

Matching and Greensted

Some two miles down the Chelmsford Road from Hatfield Heath there is a tiny lane signposted rather shyly to Matching Church (*opposite*). It bends round a little lake, probably a fish pond dug out in medieval times when the little settlement had to be self-sufficient, in fish as in meat and grain. Yet another bend in the lane reveals Matching Hall on its own little island surrounded by a moat. Its walls mantled with roses, and at its feet rushes, turn the moat into winding waterways for all kinds of

water fowl. Beautiful as that moat is, it was excavated by the Saxons purely as a defence against sudden attack. Continuous occupation of the site is shown in the Tudor barn and the charming fishing hut put up at the same time. An oak tree across the way, now large enough to block the further view, was planted to celebrate Queen Victoria's Diamond Jubilee in 1897.

Further on a humble enough row of two-storeyed cottages abutting on the churchyard is a restored survival of medieval times – a Wedding Feast House, with the upper storey all one room, originally given over for use by any parishioner in entertaining relatives and friends to a wedding feast. Such a boon it must have been, provided by a benefactor who is only vaguely remembered now as one, Mr Chimney!

What place in Essex is more redolent of a thousand years of Christian belief than St Andrew's (*inset*) at Greensted-juxta-Ongar? Miller Christy, erstwhile archaeologist wrote: 'Although it has been several times restored, it is believed to be the original structure erected as a temporary resting-place for the body of St Edmond on its way from London to Bury St Edmonds in 1013 …' But later tests have shown that it was built around AD 750.

Amidst the turmoil of our times one can stand at the church door and be back in time with those Saxon settlers who with all the reverence of their newly-adopted religion built their church from the material God had provided all around them – the great Essex forest.

Willingale

What is more inviting than a long straight road under a summer sky? The lane (*inset*) leads to the charming Willingale villages west of Chelmsford. A surprising sight awaits us – two churches standing side by side in one churchyard. They serve the separate parishes of Willingale Doe and Willingale Spain. There were days when it was possible to stand in that churchyard of a summer's evening and hear evensong in full flow on either hand. There is a lovely legend, quite untrue, that the churches were built to the order of two sisters, rivals even in religion. That is put out of court by the evidence, structurally and historically, of the differing dates of their construction.

St Christopher's, serving Willingale Doe, is to the north of the joint churchyard and goes back to the 14th century, though much restored; the north aisle belongs altogether to a thoroughgoing restoration of 1853 but the brasses go all the way back to 1442 and the memorial to Thomas Torrell represents him as a knight with all his trappings. From the 17th century, the Wisemans, the local ruling family, are represented by suitably large monuments.

St Christopher's striking battlemented tower with its diagonal buttresses rather overshadows its older neighbour, St Andrew's, but the old church can boast its longevity with Norman walls, windows and a doorway. Its chancel is nearly 500 years old. An even older feature is the door on the north side with curiously complicated ironwork going right back to the 12th century.

Until it was bought as a private residence in recent

years, the Bell, opposite and more or less between the two churches, was a popular local pub. The old landlord had his stock joke to all newcomers as he pointed across the road, 'Look there, two churches – and only one Bell between 'em!'

Duke's farmhouse (*opposite*), out here 'in the sticks' as one might say, reminds us that in medieval times the commonest material for building, found readily to hand, was the great forest which was the timberyard as well as the larder for Essex man. The skill of those builders of wooden-framed houses makes them monuments to man's medieval mastery of this natural material. Duke's is a good example of such 15th-century building – and is still lived in!

Writtle and Roxwell

The village green at Writtle is most attractive. Wide-spreading, tree-lined on the roadside, it gives access across it to the church on one hand and to three hostelries on the other. The village street takes the Chelmsford road on to Ongar, but here is a chance to sit with a drink and size up the village. Most of the old shops which overlooked the green have had to change their use in these modern times, but with little alteration in the street architecture they stay in harmony with the village atmosphere. The church of All Saints is reached through an alleyway on the far side of the green. The fine ring of bells makes mellow music on Sundays and wedding days and draws campanologists from miles around. When the

old tower was blown down in a very high wind in 1802 a local builder seized the chance to rob the ruins and build two houses on the other side of the green, which have survived to these modern times of radio and television. Appropriately mentioned, because it was here, in a little hut at the end of the village, through St John's Green, that Marconi's wireless transmission researchers sent out their first public broadcasts to the growing band of radio 'hams' on 14th February 1922.

A great attraction is the village pond (*opposite*) at the lower end of the green. It is still a real source of entertainment for children and for travellers from Chelmsford – feeding the wide range of water birds which gather, and just 'mucking about' with boats and nets.

Roxwell is such a pleasant, sleepy old place (*inset*). Modernity has passed it by, village shops have all but disappeared, leaving The Street peaceful and serene on a sunny day. But it was not so peaceful in 1901, when tragedy overtook the mill.

The mill's power source had switched from the Roxwell Brook to a Victorian steam engine. It was so dependable! But then one morning in that year the boiler exploded, bits of it landing 60 feet down the village street. Thankfully, no one was injured and it was repaired and worked through the first half of the 20th century, before lack of trade caused its conversion into a house in 1950. The old clapboard timber walls were sandwiched between two thick skins of concrete – that is why the doors and windows appear irregular to modern eyes: they are simply the original openings in that old mill.

Pleshey

There is no doubt about it, Pleshey is one of the best-kept villages I have ever seen. It gathers in such a homely way round the mound and the moat, like chicks under a hen.

The grand castle, built largely of wood, is long since gone. Even in Shakespeare's day it was 'empty lodgings and unfurnish'd walls', as he mentions in *Richard II*, Act I. The huge grassy castle mound is still there, though, made from the excavation of the deep moat (*inset*) all around it. As to that castle, we should remember that it was wholly built of wood from the forest and dated by the experts to the middle of the 12th century. Men as famous as the Mandevilles, the de Bohuns and even Thomas of Woodstock, Duke of Gloucester, owned this place in their turn and crossed the bridge over the moat many a time. It has been most sympathetically restored in recent times and now the moat and mound are the only reminders of Pleshey castle's forgotten glory.

Down in the village the great variety of cottages, from thatch and plaster to brick and tile, all so well preserved, with pretty gardens all down the street, make as colourful a background to English and Essex history as one could wish for. Today Pleshey in the sunshine could grace the jacket of a book entitled 'Britain At Its Best'. It also has a special place in history – Pleshey Lodge farm was, in the 1870s, the place where H. C. Darby's amazing 'steam digger' was first given a trial. Mr Darby had the village blacksmith produce parts of its mechanism at the forge.

Great and Little Waltham

Great Waltham is great for two reasons – one, it is bigger than its neighbour Little Waltham (*inset*), and the other is that, in area, it is one of the largest villages in the county. It includes hamlets with intriguing names like Broads Green, Littley End, Ringtail Green and Ford End. The central feature, standing right on the corner of a fierce bend in the main road, must be the church of St Mary and St Lawrence with its strong western tower, reinforced later with brick buttresses. Inside see the beautifully carved figures of angels on the ends of its hammerbeam roof.

There are many old houses in this large parish. Nikolaus Pevsner says of Langleys, north-east of the church and practically on the bank of the River Chelmer: 'The house is, in every detail, in a perfect state of preservation and upkeep. The Lodge at the entrance to the avenue which leads toward the house is to an amusing degree a miniature version of the house itself.' But why was one particular house called the Guildhall (*opposite*)? History and its spokesmen are strangely silent. It is only in recent times that it has been so lovingly restored to its old dignity.

And what is the name of the hamlet which separates Great Waltham from its Little neighbour across the river? It is called Minnow End – how appropriate!

Danbury and Margaretting

If you've ever ridden a bicycle in Essex you will have appreciated, or even blessed perhaps, the hill which rises up against the poor cyclist approaching Danbury (*opposite*) from Chelmsford on the A414. Patches of green on the OS map show us that there are still remnants of that old Essex forest lingering all around the village. Durrant's *Handbook to Essex* of 1887 declares: 'This, perhaps the most delightfully situated parish in the county, lies entirely on and around the summit of Danbury Hill … whence a charming view may be had …'

Its name is not a reminder of Danish intrusion, it comes from a Saxon tribe who made this place their stronghold.

By the time of the Domesday Book (1086) it was vested in the Norman knight Geoffrey de Mandeville, the Earl of Essex. By the 15th century it was in the hands of the D'Arcy family, but a century later Sir William Mildmay was calling it home, and he it was who built Danbury Place which, according to the Hearth Tax return of 1662 had 22 fireplaces. It was bought by John Round in 1831. He had it demolished and built the present house in its place. It was sold again in 1892 and over ten years the owner had 429 oak trees cut down and sold for timber. Now Danbury Park, its buildings and its surroundings, is safely in the hands of Essex County Council. During the Second World War it served as a War Emergency Hospital, giving many East End mothers-to-be a safe refuge for the birth of their babies.

The Griffin up the hill and on the other side of the road can claim that Joseph Strutt, historian and novelist was writing a novel in his room there when he died. Sir Walter Scott finished it – and published it under his own name! This old inn is now a popular meeting-and-eating rendezvous.

Margaretting, a beautiful name for a village, derives from the dedication of the parish church to St Margaret. With through traffic taking the A12(T) round the village on its way to London, the village and the hinterland north and south are still pastoral. The village sign (*inset*), right on the brink of the village pond, was carved in wood and painted by craftsman Harry Carter of Swaffham. It was paid for with funds accruing from the Queen's Silver Jubilee celebrations and erected in 1977.

Tollesbury Marina and Tolleshunt D'Arcy

I like Tollesbury, the village, the lonely marshes, the wild life. It is appreciated, too, by scores of 'yachties' who come here to tie up for a week or a winter in calm waters with all mod cons to hand.

In 1868 an Act of Parliament established a company's right to no fewer than 350 acres from here down to Maldon for their oyster fishery. Ten years later the Tollesbury and Blackwater Fishery had another large area laid down to oyster beds; their harvest being sent as far away as Russia. The sail lofts for servicing their boats have been splendidly restored, in timber frames and clapboard walls. They are an unusual and obvious landmark. Today, though, you can best savour the flavour of the place by walking round the marina and then to the village itself which grows ever bigger as the delights of sea and sky and 'just mucking about in boats' catch a wider imagination.

Not so many people now can recall a journey on the light railway which ran from here to join the main line at Kelvedon. It took the fishermen's oysters far and wide and got the local nickname of the Crab and Winkle line. Opened in 1904, it was extended right down to the sea wall three years later when a pier was built. It has now passed into history, as the last privately financed rail-sea link to be introduced into this country.

At the junction of the B1023 and the B1026 there stands a monument most redolent of a vanished village way of life – the Victorian maypole of Tolleshunt D'Arcy with an unusual white-painted wooden 'cage' around its base. Without the sight and smell of modern traffic we could well be back in those May days when the old rites associated with the fertility of spring were celebrated in merry dancing – and not a little flirting.

Just a little down the street at D'Arcy House, Dr Salter, the village doctor, lived for over 60 years into the 1930s, dispensing medicine and homely advice to folk over an area far wider than this village. He was followed in that same house by Margery Allingham, the famous detective story writer.

Tolleshunt D'Arcy Hall still preserves its ancient moat with a four-arched Elizabethan bridge, while the Hall itself, built at the beginning of the 16th century keeps company with the church of St Nicholas (*inset*). That was restored in 1897, but some of the brasses go back 500 years and more, like the D'Arcy family monuments; one of them a brass about four feet long.

Cressing

Every year at Cressing there is a big plant sale organised by the Red Cross Society. It is held, in October, in two barns which stand as evidence of man's ingenuity a thousand years ago. They keep company with the farmhouse in beautiful, well-kept grounds including a delightful walled garden planted in Tudor Paradisal style.

The land and the barns were first in the keeping of the Order of Knights Templars in 1135. The Templars and similar orders came and went, the farm and its buildings passed into the hands of private owners and, fortunately for us, those two amazingly large barns with their vast mellow-tiled roofs were preserved. They have been dated by the experts to about the year 1000 in the case of the Barley Barn, and sometime in the 13th century for the Wheat Barn (*opposite*), the largest, which is some 120 feet long and 40 feet high. Together they make a landmark just off the B1018, Witham Road, about three miles south of Braintree, where the road and the Essex Way run together. The Essex Way continues on right by the barns. The site is open from Easter to October, Monday to Friday. An exhibition in one of the barns traces the history of these amazing survivors through 750 years of our turbulent island story.

After that the parish church of All Saints has little to offer by way of comparison, but the natural beauty of the countryside, farmed as the seasons change is an inspiration in itself. The name of the place, Cressing – 'The place where the cress grows' – conjures up a delightful vision in the imagination.

Terling and Fairstead

There's a shocking tragedy to be recounted which happened amidst the beautiful tranquillity of Terling (*opposite*). First the beauty. Where to begin? Pevsner tells us: 'The village is specially attractive.' That remark will be echoed most sincerely by anybody who has seen the grouping, the church in its green churchyard and the River Ter splashing down into a wide pool below the village while the unusual sundial shadows the time up on the mellow brick tower of All Saints.

Terling Place has been the home of the Strutt family since it was built in 1765. The Lords Rayleigh have been famous in the spheres of literature, science and agriculture.

The third Baron Rayleigh (1842–1919) won the Nobel prize for physics in 1904.

Such a peaceful scene does not seem the likely stage for a disaster, but there was one, a tragedy enacted in the old smock mill, half a mile to the west. In 1950, Herbert Bonner, at the age of 78, was still giving his son Leslie a hand at busy times. On a day when a tractor was driving the machinery by belt from a shed at ground level, Herbert climbed up to the top of the mill for some reason now unknown and slipped somehow into the great train of cogs that turned the spur-wheel. His cries of agony were heard by workers on the ground, but the old miller's weight prevented them from reversing the drive to release him before he had died a most painful death. And to think that this mill was used in 1937 for a film comedy starring Will Hay, when stunt men were swung round on the sails!

Get the flavour of Fairstead even today from dear old Miller Christy's *Handbook for Essex* published over 100 years ago! 'The church (St Mary) is a quaint and ancient building of Early English age, the tower and chancel being especially pure and having lancet windows. In the basement of the tower which is partly built of Roman brick, are a huge oak chest, 9ft long, and cut out of solid timber, with many locks and bands, and an old iron charcoal pan for warming the church'.

The Saxons called this 'The fair, pleasant place', and today its fields and its farms and its homes (*inset*) reflect that judgment even after a thousand years.

Wivenhoe

It looks so peaceful on a summer's day, dreaming, you might say, of past importance. But it was not the place to be on that day in 1884 when the Great Essex Earthquake damaged many houses there, one of them Quayside Cottage, which had to be completely rebuilt. That is why that year is inscribed on its wall, for visitors to see. A metaphorical earthquake occurred in 1962 when Essex County Council bought the house and the land of Wivenhoe Park, featured in a well known painting by John Constable. That house was incorporated in the larger property designed by Thomas Hopper for the Rebow family in 1846. Now its park houses all the adjuncts needed for the new Essex University, with gaunt residential blocks, lecture rooms, laboratories, and all the shops and restaurants required in a community a good deal larger than the village itself.

Yet the view from the further bank of the River Colne (*opposite*) shows little evidence of the presence of this large modern institution. It is taken from the point where the ferry runs at appropriate times of wind and weather. This little settlement gathered round its church, which although much restored in 1860, when it was the community centre as much as the house of God, can show its earlier history in brasses with dates going back 400 years. Its tower was built around 1500 and looks as strong as the faith which first inspired its erection.

The quay has been busier, but that is a benefit to the casual visitor who can soak up a quiet view, forget life's pressing timetable and, maybe, take a seat in the window of the Rose and Crown (*inset*), at peace with the world. There would still be time to stroll round to East Street and admire the old Essex art of pargeting seen in all its glory on the front of Garrison House. But let's leave that till after a good lunch in the Rose and Crown, right in front of us!

Arkesden and Saffron Walden

Arkesden (*opposite*) is a pretty village, with delightful houses round the green beside a little stream, a winter bourne called Wicken Water. Narrow lanes under big trees

give open views across the wide fields. With a history going back thousands of years, Arkesden boasts several interesting buildings including Wood Hall (the manor house), a Tudor dwelling 'Becketts' and the fascinating church of St Mary the Virgin.

In the mid 19th century, when the church was being extensively restored and the present west tower built, traces of a Norman tower were discovered. Amongst the many monuments that grace the interior is an impressive memorial of 1592 to Richard Cutte and his wife.

Saffron Walden is also steeped in history. As its very name suggests, it once thrived on the saffron crocus that was grown here in medieval times for its gorgeous yellow dye as well as for cooking purposes. On the eastern end of the Common, a more ancient symbol can be found. The grass maze (*inset*) is claimed to be the best earthen maze still surviving in England. It covers a circle of about 100 feet in diameter with concentric circles cut in the turf around a centrepiece of raised earth. It is thought to have been trodden by a prehistoric tribe as part of a religious fertility rite. It is easy to imagine their frenzied dancing as they beseeched the gods to look favourably on their crops.

Ugley

So it is called, but there is no evidence here of ugliness. In fact this charming village gets its name from the Old English, indicating that this was Ucga's nook, where this Saxon leader brought his little tribe to settle in the great

forest which then covered much of Essex. Here they set up their camp, chopped down trees to make a clearance and used them to build more permanent homes and their communal 'hall' where Ucga and his henchmen would have laid their heads. On that same spot, and down the years, the village of Ugley developed. Ugley Hall would have evolved from that 'chief's barracks' as we might call it. Orford House, a mile to the south of the church, was transformed from that old hall into a home to suit a noble lord around 1700.

It's summer and time for the village fete. The grass has been mown and the table and chairs set up outside the cottages. The tea and other beverages, hot and cold, are all ready in urns, jugs and pots, and folk are sitting there in anticipation of the usual goodies the fete produces every year, thanks to a lot of voluntary help which started weeks ago. The sun is shining, the crops are ripening, all's right with the world. Our much-loved and lamented Poet Laureate, John Betjeman catches the mood in his poem *Essex*:

> The deepest Essex few explore,
> Where steepest thatch is sunk in flowers
> And out of elms and sycamore
> Rise flinty fifteenth century towers …

Henham-on-the-Hill and Elsenham

Shortened, of course, in these rush-and-tear days to just plain Henham, its full name sounds, somehow, as poetically pastoral as its position out in the Essex countryside, 34 miles from London, 6 miles north-east from Elsenham, and the same distance and direction from Bishops Stortford. The last county directory of Essex, published in 1937, is a voice from the past itself, saying: '... the church of St Mary the Virgin is a large and ancient building of stone in the Perpendicular style, consisting of chancel, nave ... south porch and an embattled western tower with short spire, containing 5 bells and a clock placed there in 1887 ... an ancient oak screen divides the chancel and the nave; ... the land is mainly owned by farmers ... The soil is partly gravel and strong clay and loam. The crops are wheat, oats, barley, sugar beet, roots and beans ... the population in 1931 was 695.'

Over 60 years later Henham (*opposite*) is still a very beautiful, undeveloped village. Even Nikolaus Pevsner, the architectural scholar, has to add to his description of the place a reference to the 'especially pretty village green'.

When I was a child I badly wanted a clockwork train set to call my own. It would have a station just like that at Elsenham (*inset*), clean and bright, with a platform on which there would have been slot machines for bars of chocolate, a station master to see that everything was in order to receive the next train, a lamppost to light it up at night, and hanging baskets of pretty flowers to make it the most beautiful, tidiest, best little station in the world! That dream was resurrected when I visited Elsenham, as I remembered John Betjeman's evocative lines from *Essex*:

> I saw the little branch line go
> By white farms roofed in red and brown,
> The old Great Eastern winding slow
> To some forgotten country town.

Audley End and Newport

Audley End on the outskirts of Saffron Walden boasts a wonderful Jacobean house (*opposite*). It was originally built for Thomas Howard, 1st Earl of Suffolk (1561–1626) who had married Margaret Audley, daughter of the Lord Chancellor. When Howard was appointed to

the office of Lord Treasurer, King James visited Audley End and was so amazed by the scale of it that he quipped, 'By my troth, man, it is too much for a king, but may do for a Lord High Treasurer!'

After a process of demolition and renovation over the centuries, the house we now see is only about half the original but retains a wealth of architecture. The gardens and grounds were designed by Robert Adam and 'Capability' Brown and today provide a superb setting for a summer game of cricket.

Thirty years ago D. I. Gordon wrote *A Brief History of the Village of Newport* – a slim volume which has become a collector's item. It gallops from pre-Saxon times to the Great War, so I was pleased to get confirmation of my own researches. The first church built by the Saxons was replaced by 1240 to give the basic plan of the present place of worship, but the next two centuries of further building brought about a very large church, indicative of the wealth of the leading inhabitants who had benefited from the trade which the main road brought to local industries, farmers and tradesmen. Those farmers were fortunate to have a very fertile soil to provide crops for food and grazing for animals.

In the middle of the village is an ancient house called Monk's Barn, the exterior wall of which (*inset*) bears a carving of the Coronation of the Blessed Virgin. My old *Kelly's Directory* of Essex tells me: 'this house belonged to the Monks of St Martin-in-the-Fields, and was used by them as a sanatorium.'

Thaxted

Once a market town, for pigs and poultry, held every Friday in the yard of the Swan Hotel, Thaxted still attracts visitors through its beautiful church (*opposite*) and its old buildings and its position in verdant Essex countryside. Hamlets gather round like chicks round a hen: Monk Street, Bardfield End Green, Cutlers Green, Richmonds Green, Sibleys Green; all calling for our attention when there is already enough to intrigue and delight us in Thaxted itself.

Look at the Guildhall, for example, at the upper end of Town Street (*inset*). It has been standing there for over 500 years, just like the Recorder's House nearby. Let the expert Nikolaus Pevsner sum the place up: 'the town as a whole is very perfect, chiefly because there is truly not one house in it that would appear violently out of place.'

To Thaxted Spire

Majestic giant! Lordly Spire!
What joys thy aspect doth inspire,
When absent long from home and thee,
Thy towering beacon first I see!

Thy glittering vane (seen many a mile),
Proclaims my welcome with a smile:
And tells of home and evening fire,
Not far from thee, dear Thaxted Spire!

… And I would wish, whene'er I die,
Beneath thy shade in peace to lie,
And greet, when human joys expire
Thine hallow'd precincts – Thaxted Spire!

'J.T.'

Finchingfield

'The country life is to be preferred, for there we see the works of God … The country is both the philosopher's garden and his library … A sweet and natural retreat from noise and talk, and allows opportunity for reflection, and gives the best subjects for it.'

William Penn, *Some Fruits of Solitude* (1644–1718).

Surely Finchingfield must be the Calendar Queen of Essex! The view is usually from the village pond, a very large one, looking up the hill to the church. But there are other facets of the Finchingfield story to be revealed – the windmill, Spains Hall and, of course, the church with the Guildhall next door to it.

Windmills were a common sight in this village. K. G. Farries' book, *Essex Windmills, Millers and Millwrights*, in five volumes, tells us about them in full detail. All eight of them! Long after they were active flour-producers they stayed on, gradually crumbling – beautiful landmarks in the history of man's ingenuity. The one at Duck End, or Town Street, (*inset*) just north of the village centre has been taken under the wing of Essex County Council, so its preservation is assured.

The winter scene of this pretty place has all the appeal of a Christmas card. The parish church of St John thrusts its Norman tower above the houses. Inside there's a memorial to William Kempe, who died in 1628. He made a vow never to utter a word for seven years after he had a row with his wife and accused her of being unfaithful, when he knew that she had always been constant and true. The legend goes that at his home, Spains Hall, he had his workmen dig out a pond for each year of that vow completed. Alas, he died before the vow expired.

The Rodings

These have been summed up so well by Miller Christy back in 1903: 'To all except hunting men, the large district of Essex now known as 'The Roothings' but formerly as 'the Rodings' is a veritable *terra incognita*. The eight (formerly nine) small parishes composing the district take their common name from the River Roding which flows through their midst. They are Abbess Roothing, Aythorpe Roothing, Beauchamp, Berners and High Roothing, Leaden Roothing, Margaret, White and Morell Roothing. The last is now incorporated with White Roothing. As old Norden, writing in 1594, says quaintly: "The Roding first appeareth nere Takely, whence as she passeth she greeteth her nine daughters, all the Rodings." All are thinly populated and purely rural … They are neither intersected nor approached by any important main road; they contain no ancient earthwork, no picturesque ruin, no large church, not even a single monumental brass and no residence of greater consequence than a large farmhouse or country parsonage. No district so near London (and the nearest portion of the Roothings lies within twenty-five miles of St Paul's) is so little known.'

Despite the bustle and noise of traffic through the village streets today, that atmosphere can still be captured by the percipient visitor. At Aythorpe Roding the white, weather-boarded post mill (*opposite*) still makes an ideal scene for the photographer. High Roding, on the High Way, a main road even in early days, is virtually a one-street village. Its old inn, the Black Lion (*inset*) was offering food and drink and lodging beyond human memory. Miller Christy may well have dropped in there for refreshment on his tour of the Rodings.

High Easter and Good Easter

Back in the days when local post offices postmarked the mail they handled, people would travel miles at Eastertide to get cards franked 'Good Easter' or 'High Easter'. Actually, Easter was entered as Estre or Ester in court records as far back as 1017 and as Godystre by 1208. Experts have interpreted this as 'sheepfold' with connection to a woman, 'Godiva'. After a thousand years of development both these 'Easter' villages remain as beautiful reminders of a vanished way of life.

Good Easter (*inset*) is a photographer's dream. The

church of St Andrew shows the care bestowed on it by Christians in the parish from its building, its repair and its renewal through more than 700 years. The south porch reminds us of an essential part of the marriage ceremony 500 years ago. Long before the common folk could write their own names, the confirmation of the solemn contract of marriage was signified at the church door by the exchange of rings. A porch was added to keep the happy couple dry during this crucial part of the ceremony, and benches were placed in it for the seating of the necessary witnesses. Only later in history was the ring ceremony added to the service conducted in the church.

Good Easter's twin sister, High Easter, (*opposite*) reflects the passage of time in this beautiful corner of the county. The old windmill there, arms amputated, has become a prestigious home, offering grand views from its high windows. Round the corner new houses have replaced the old blacksmith's shop right on the village street. But not before it was fully photographed as it was on the day the blacksmith left it with all the tools lying about – and went home to die. Those photographs and those tools are safely preserved in the Chelmsford and Essex Museum as a tribute to one of the most important men in Essex villages through more than 800 years. Derek Bircher, former grocer to the village, has kept such memories green in his *One Village in History*.

Little Easton and Dunmow

Little Easton (*opposite*) was the home of Frances Evelyn Maynard, who married the 5th Earl of Warwick in 1881. At court she was a friend of the Prince of Wales, the future King Edward VII. Her monument in St Mary's tells part of the story: 'Frances Evelyn Maynard, Countess of Warwick, Lady of the Manor of Estaines (Easton), Born December 10, 1861. Died July 26, 1938.'

Her connection with Little Easton lives on in the now restored gardens around Manor House, comprising a group of 17th-century timber-framed houses with a wing built a century later, a detached large house of the 18th century and a barn close by.

The church, dedicated to St Mary, still shows indications of its Norman origin. One of its wall-paintings has been dated, expertly, to as early as 1175 and there are others dated through into the 15th century. There's much here at which to stand and gaze in awe.

Great and Little Dunmow unite in the ceremony of the Flitch of Bacon, celebrated every Leap Year. The bacon is presented to any married couple who can …

> '… swear by custom of confession
> That you ne'er made nuptial transgression:
> Nor since you were married man and wife,
> By household brawls or contentious strife,
> Or otherwise, at bed or board,
> Offended each other in deed or word:
> Or, since the parish clerk said, 'Amen',
> Wished yourselves unmarried again.'

This ancient custom was introduced following the founding of a priory at Little Dunmow in 1104. At a 'trial' before local worthies the most convincing couple were presented with the flitch and carried on wooden chairs on men's shoulders in a noisy and merry procession. Though the ceremony fell into abeyance in 1751, it has been revived in our time, transferred to Great Dunmow and suitably updated for present circumstances and audiences. In the church of St Mary at Little Dunmow there is still kept one of those first chairs (*inset*), actually made from part of a 13th-century stall.

Felsted

Old, beautiful and educational – that's Felsted, with just a little joke to add to the mixture. The joke needs a reference to the Domesday Book, compiled by 1086. In that book under the entry for Felsted there is a naughty Norman knight holding land in the parish whose name is written down for all to see as: 'Roger God-save-the-ladies'!

Now for more serious matters, like the amazing monument in the parish church of the Holy Cross (*opposite*), raised to the memory of the first Lord Rich who died in 1568 and his son who died in 1581, but strangely not erected until around 1620. It stands against the wall showing a life-sized figure of Lord Rich reclining on a couch looking at his son who is kneeling, facing a prayer desk.

The way to the church is through the passage under the old house with an overhanging upper storey, all painted white under a mellow, tiled roof (*inset*). This was the old School House where began that first school founded by Lord Rich, which is now in far greater and grander premises as Felsted School – a world-famous private establishment.

Amongst all the old buildings which make a walk about the place so pleasant there is one which bears the message on its bressumer: 'George Boote made this, 1596.' I wonder if succeeding generations of Bootes have come back to Felsted to look with pride on that house and inscription?

At Felsted's village, neat and small
Whose church-tower rises grey and tall,
Still stands an ancient dwelling there,
Of strange device and carving rare.
Now partly lost 'neath patch and paint.
Retaining still a legend quaint,
In letters old with grand parade
Which tell by whom THIS HOUSE WAS MADE.

George T. Manning, *Rural Rhymes* (1837)

Coggeshall

Of course, the sight that every tourist looks for here is the house built 500 years ago for Thomas Paycocke in West Street (*opposite*): 'one of the most attractive half-timbered houses of England regardless of the fact that much of its façade is restored ...', says the architectural expert. If one looks at the bressumer, the main beam of the overhanging upper storey, one can appreciate the delightful carving which includes the incorporation of Thomas Paycocke's initials. It is now a National Trust property and open to the public through summer mid-week afternoons.

Coggeshall has bridges over the Blackwater, which does a sharp right-hand turn through the village. The old bridge south of the village centre is the Long Bridge, a perfect place to take children to feed the birds which swim up or fly in at the first throw of a few crumbs.

The bridge which catches one's imagination, though, used these days by just a few villagers, is the graceful 'iron bridge' made by Dick Nunn outside his smithy in 1892. Then, many workers used a footpath through the fields to get to work on distant farms as well as for a leisurely riverside walk. Dick the Smith was a great local character with a mind of his own. When the parish council would not replace the rotting old wooden bridge which was a real danger, he made one of iron at his own expense, assembling it all down the side of his forge, 30 feet long and wide enough for two people abreast. A grand opening ceremony was held after it had been manhandled to the river all across the fields on two trollies. The 703 people who crossed Nunn's Bridge on that day sounded Dick's praises for this engineering achievement and for his generosity.

Just to the north of Coggeshall are the colourful Marks Hall Gardens (*inset*), fashioned from part of the Markshall Estate, home of the Honeywood family in the 17th century. Part of the gardens is set aside as a memorial to the RAF and the United States Army Air Force.

Pebmarsh

Pebmarsh. Where is it? Just over three miles north of Earls Colne and four miles north-west of Halstead. It took two and a half centuries for this village to get anything like a commonly accepted name. Old records quote it as Bebenters in the Domesday Book of 1086 and Pubemers in the 12th century. Not till the 16th century does it appear in written form as Pedmarche and so at last to its modern name. It has come a long way from the Old English name for 'Pybba's stubble-field', and we would not have known that but for the scholarship of P. H. Reany and his *Place-Names of Essex* (1935).

This village still preserves the pastoral air engendered by its name, yet at the end of the 18th century it was the site of a factory – a textile mill! When George Courtauld and his wife Ruth returned to England after 15 years in the United States they settled here, in 1798, where George and his partner, one Mr Whipps set up a silk-weaving factory. It has been said that in 1896 he had a factory built, as well as homes for his workers. Then he moved on and up to greater things. You could say that in terms of local jobs Pebmarsh was the loser but it also meant that Pebmarsh retained much of its rural charm. The water mill that drove Courtauld's looms was demolished at the beginning of the 20th century but the pretty timber-framed and plastered millhouse is still lived in.

The King's Head (*opposite*) has been a popular hostelry for time out of mind, entered in the earliest directories. The church of St John the Baptist is coming up to 700 years old! It is rather strange to see that the 14th-century west tower was completed more than a hundred years later in red brick. At the same time a porch in the same red brick was added on the south side. The outstanding feature inside is the brass (*inset*), one of the most significant in the county, celebrating the life of Sir William Fitzralph who died early in the 13th century. It shows a knight in full armour in the typical crossed-legs pose of memorials of the day.

Castle Hedingham

A beautiful large village – some of its inhabitants would call it a town – standing in the shadow of that castle up above them on its mound. Its keep is a fascinating place to visit for it gives us a picture of life in Essex as it was lived in the 12th century when a grand castle was built here to the order of the de Veres, Earls of Oxford, one of the most powerful and most famous families of those Norman times. It stands proudly on a rise above the village; complete enough to be impressive on all sides, especially when one enters and sees the great arch spanning a large room from east to west (*inset*).

Among the minor delights which show homely aspects of everyday life in Norman times are the narrow recesses

in the castle wall which, of necessity, are partitioned off today; they were the 'garde robes' or primitive toilets used by the early occupiers, of all ranks. The ordure simply dropped from all the floors to the cellars of the keep so that it could be cleared out from time to time, to be loaded onto a cart and dumped in the moat. No doubt the same place from which they caught the fish for dinner! Lifting that particular curtain of history makes us grateful for modern sanitation enjoyed in our more humble homes.

The church down in the dip below the castle, suffers from comparison with that aged, massive bulk but it, too, has greensward to set off its architecture (*opposite*); with a tall, square tower in brick, apparently restored in 1616 to its former glory, with stepped battlements and supported by big, diagonally placed buttresses with a little stair turret over-topping them. On the walls of the aisle the battlements are also of brick and so is the clerestory. On those walls are emblems of the de Veres, a frieze of shields, and, over the clerestory windows, a star. Pevsner says that from the interior it can be seen that this is one of 'the most ambitiously designed in Essex. A complete Late Norman parish church'. The chancel is really extravagant in its ornamentation, while the double hammerbeam roof of the nave is one of only four of its kind in Essex. There are other interesting details like the misericords of the chancel seats or 'stalls', with carvings including a wolf carrying off a monk, a fox with a distaff, a man's face and other conceits, amusing and beautifully executed.

Manningtree and Mistley Quay

With all the building which has been going on in recent times, Manningtree (*opposite*) could be losing its identity as a 'large village'. It has to be admitted however that, as early as 1887, Durrant's *Handbook to Essex* calls it 'a considerable market town' on the south bank of the Stour. But with the passing of the years the market, with its trade in corn, malt, timber, fish and so on faded away and new light industries replaced the big maltings, though some of them still remain, tall monuments of past prosperity in a changing world.

Memory lingers long in a local community and Matthew Hopkins is still talked about by Manningtree historians. He lived in the 17th century and became obsessed by the idea that witches were alive and well and living not just in Manningtree but all over Essex and beyond. He blamed them, poor innocent old ladies, for all the tragedies and misfortunes, deaths and disasters which affected villages and larger communities. His stature as a practising lawyer made him trusted and believed. In 1644 he obtained a commission from Parliament to go on a witch-hunt around Manningtree and much further afield. Within a year he had 200 people arrested, of whom 68 were executed by hanging or burning just on his word alone. So the 'Witchfinder General' gave the whole area around Manningtree a bad name!

Durrant's *Handbook* goes on: 'The Corn Exchange, in High Street is of stone and was built in 1865 … the church was erected in 1616, but has been twice enlarged. It is architecturally a miserable building …' Well that is the view of one person over a hundred years ago. Today I would say that the wider view is charming with the broad waters

of the Stour as a backcloth to the varied townscape of buildings old and new and, on the water, the myriad swans in grey youth or white adult purity waiting for the titbits which people cannot resist offering.

From very early times, Mistley prospered owing to its position on the river Stour. In the 18th century, a new village was built with brick houses, granaries, warehouses, a large malting office and quays (*inset*). This was all due to the efforts of Richard Rigby, M.P. who also had designs to turn the place into a spa.

Dedham

One authority has claimed for it the accolade: 'Most attractive small town in Essex'. Few of the thousands of tourists who make Dedham a 'must' on their schedule of places to visit would disagree.

It is noticeable that the Constable connection has not led to 'Constable Tea Rooms' or other commercialisation of that ilk, though, of course, Essex is proud of its link with the great landscape painter, John Constable, whose works are part of our national heritage. He was not born here but daily he crossed the bridge over the River Stour to come to school here, and later celebrated his connection with the place in great paintings like *Dedham Vale* and *Dedham Lock* in the early years of the 19th century. The picture probably decorating more homes than any other work of art is *The Haywain* which eventually found its rightful place in the National Gallery. The 'Lock', on the Stour, was part of the Stour Navigation from Sudbury to the sea. It is featured in the painting popularly known as *The Leaping Horse* of 1825.

But let us go back to the village street overlooked by the church (*opposite*), where buildings of all ages live in harmony, no doubt because they still perform their functions as shops, inns and houses. There are two houses of about 1730 once used for the Grammar School, but now owned by the National Trust and so well-maintained right up to the unusual sundial, high on the parapet. Woe betide the schoolboy who ignored that relentless moving shadow! In the 17th century it belonged to a clothier, Edward Sherman, who established the first school here, later amalgamated with the older Grammar School.

The River Stour marks the boundary between Essex and Suffolk from Sturmer to its estuary. Here, just a short walk along the Stour Valley Path we can look back to Bridge Cottage and the Constable family's mill at Flatford. And, across the river, is the famous Willy Lott's cottage (*inset*). Graced by the many swans and the rustic scenery, this is a memory which any traveller will cherish.

It is easy to underestimate the beauty of Essex. With its commuter-belt image and flat landscape, many are tempted to overlook its finer qualities. However, Essex is a county to be proud of and cherished. And, for those who are visitors, there is much to see and explore. Through the images of expert photographer, Robert Hallmann, and the commentary of local author, Stan Jarvis, this book celebrates the county in all its glory.

Robert Hallmann has lived in Essex for most of his life. His first major photographic exhibition was in London in 1978. Since then he has won a number of local and national competitions and was runner-up in a Kobal–*Independent on Sunday* Portrait Competition with an exhibition at the National Portrait Gallery. His illustrated books include *The British Landscape, Coastal Britain* and *The Beauty of England*.

Stan Jarvis has lived in Chelmsford for over fifty years. He has contributed numerous articles to local newspapers and magazines; has regularly broadcast on local radio; and is the author of over twenty books on local history, including *Essex: A County History*.

Front cover photograph:
ST OSYTH QUAY
Back cover photograph:
BARNSTON